The Jewish Cookbook for Everyone

Jewish Meals Are A Cultural Tradition

Table of Contents

Introduction 4

Appetizers 6

    Chopped Liver 7

    Knish 9

    Smoked Whitefish Dip 12

    Reuben Dip 14

Breads 16

    Challah 17

    Bagels 20

    Jewish Rye Bread 23

    Cinnamon Bread 26

Main Meals 29

    Beef Brisket 30

    Kosher Cholent Recipe 32

    Prime Rib 35

    Slow Cooker Pot Roast 38

    Roasted Chicken 40

    Cornish Game Hens 43

    Turkey Breast in the Slow Cooker 46

    Stuffed Breast of Veal 48

    Breaded Veal Chops 51

Soups and Stews *53*

    Matzo Ball Soup 54

    Chicken Chili 57

    Sweet and Sour Cabbage Soup 59

    Lentil Soup 61

Seafood *63*

    Glazed Salmon 64

    Halibut with Walnut Coating 66

    Exotic Shabbat Fish 68

Sides *70*

    Roasted Cauliflower 71

    Cheese Blintzes 73

    Passover Haroset 76

    Potato Latkes 78

    Beans and Artichoke Salad 80

    Herring Salad 82

Dessert *84*

    Rugelach 85

    Chocolate Torte 88

    Apple Bundt Cake 91

    Kugel 94

    Honey Cake 96

Introduction

There is no one correct Jewish cuisine. Orthodox Jews following strict eating and cooking guidelines for kosher meals. Jews who are more secular-oriented may follow the rules less ardently. They usually feel comfortable eating out in a non-kosher environment. Many wholly secular Jews celebrate holidays more for cultural reasons than religious ones.

Whatever their eating habits, Jewish cooking follows a long and ancient tradition. Jewish recipes, usually of Ashkenazy or Sephardic heritage, uniquely tell the story of Jewish history through time. It is a cultural journey as well as a culinary one. Meals are invariably the highlight of any holiday for even the most secular of Jews.

Regardless of their religious status, there are certain rules just about every Jew follows. No meal may combine fish or meat with dairy foods. And shellfish and pork are forbidden. Contrary to popular belief, kosher is not a type of cooking or food. It's a way of preparing a meal. A Chinese dish, following kosher standards, can be perfectly kosher.

The answer to why Orthodox Jews follow kosher rules can be a big vague. There may be some digestive benefits to not combining meat and dairy. But the real answer to kosher guidelines is that the Torah says so. It's as simple as that.

The recipes in this Jewish Cookbook adhere to the general Jewish rules. When a recipe calls for the combination of meat and dairy, we provide a non-dairy alternative. Whether you buy strictly kosher or not kosher at all is up to you.

This Jewish Cookbook provides recipes for Orthodox and secular Jews alike. They are meant to be enjoyed as a celebration of life and of a long history. And what non-Jew can resist the tasty recipes in the Jewish Cookbook?

Appetizers

Chopped Liver

A delicious appetizer served on pumpernickel bread.

Cooking Time: 12 minutes

Servings: 10

Ingredients:

- 3 lb. chicken liver
- 3 tbsp. chicken fat
- 1 chopped onion
- 2 garlic cloves

- 3 tbsp. cognac
- Salt and pepper to taste
- 2 tbsp. chopped parsley

Directions:

1. Heat the chicken fat in a skillet and sauté the onion for 5 minutes.

2. Stir in the chicken liver and sauté for 7 minutes, until the livers are no longer pink.

3. Place the chicken livers, onion and garlic in a food processor and process until smooth.

4. Transfer the mixture to a bowl and stir in the remaining ingredients.

5. Refrigerate the chopped liver for at least an hour.

Knish

Oh, that delicious mashed potato baked in dough. Perfect.

Cooking Time: 40 minutes

Servings: 50

Ingredients:

- 7 large peeled and cubed potatoes
- ¼ cup butter
- 2 chopped onions
- Salt and pepper to taste
- 3 tbsp. vegetable broth

- 2 minced garlic cloves
- 1 cup shredded cheddar cheese
- 2 eggs
- ½ butter
- ½ tsp. salt
- 4 cups white flour
- 2 egg yolks
- 3 tbsp. milk

Directions:

1. Quarter the potatoes and cook them in boiling salted water for 15 minutes, until done.

2. Drain the potatoes and set aside.

3. Heat the oil in a skillet and sauté the onions for 5 minutes.

4. Place the potatoes, onions, salt, pepper, garlic, broth and shredded cheese in a large bowl and mash well. This can be done with a hand mixer. Set aside.

5. Preheat the oven to 375 degrees.

6. Cover a baking sheet with aluminum foil.

7. Whip the eggs and oil with a cup of warm water and season with salt.

8. Slowly add the flour until you have a dough.

9. Knead the dough for about 8 minutes on a floured surface.

10. Roll out the dough and cut out 10 x 13 strips.

11. Spoon ¼ cup of filling down the center of each strip.

12. Roll up the dough and seal by pressing at the ends.

13. Cut each strip into 1-inch slices and transfer to the baking sheet.

14. Beat the egg yolk and milk and brush each slice with the mixture.

15. Bake for 40 minutes.

Smoked Whitefish Dip

Smoked whitefish is a great delicacy. Serve it up as a dip with crackers. Be aware that the combination of fish and dairy makes this non-kosher.

Cooking Time: 0

Servings: 16

Ingredients:

- 2 cups flaked and deboned smoked whitefish
- 3 tbsp. cream cheese
- ¼ cup sour cream

- ½ tsp. dill
- 1 tsp. horseradish
- Dash Worcestershire sauce

Directions:

1. Use a hand mixer to combine all ingredients except the whitefish.

2. Stir in the whitefish.

3. Serve with crackers.

Reuben Dip

This is an incredible dip. Every Jewish deli has its Reuben sandwich, but the combination of meat and dairy makes it non-kosher. For kosher, substitute a vegan cheese for the Swiss cheese. This is a terrific use for leftover corned beef

Cooking Time: 15 minutes

Servings: 12 servings

Ingredients:

- 2 cups Bavarian (sweet) sauerkraut
- 2 cups shredded Swiss cheese
- 2 cups shredded and chopped cooked corned beef
- ½ cup thousand island dressing
- ½ tsp. horseradish
- 1 tsp. Dijon mustard

Directions:

1. Combine all ingredients in a pot and simmer for 15 minutes.

2. Serve hot with cocktail rye bread.

Breads

Challah

This wonderful eggy bread makes the best French toast.

Cooking Time: 35 minutes

Servings: 25

Ingredients:

- 1 cup warm milk
- 1 ½ cup warm water
- 1 tbsp active dry yeast
- 1 cup honey

- ¼ cup canola oil
- 1 egg
- 3 egg yolks (save the egg whites)
- 1 tsp. salt
- 8 cups white flour
- 1 cup raisins

Directions:

1. Combine the water and milk with a package of active dry yeast. Let side for 10 minutes.

2. Add the honey, oil, egg, egg yolks and salt and combine well.

3. Add a cup of flour and stir after each addition.

4. Add the raisins.

5. Knead the dough until it is smooth.

6. Cover the dough with a damp towel and let rise for 1 hour.

7. Punch the dough down.

8. Flour a flat surface and pull the dough into 2 separate pieces.

9. Knead each piece for about 5 minutes.

10. Pull each half-dough piece into 3 sections and create a roll 1 ½ inches wide.

11. Braid both dough pieces.

12. Bring the 2 braids together into a round loaf and secure the ends.

13. Lightly butter a large baking tray and place the braided loaves on the tray.

14. Cover the tray with a damp towel and let rise for 45 minutes.

15. Beat the reserved egg whites and brush over the loaves.

16. Heat the oven to 375 degrees.

17. Bake for 35 minutes.

Bagels

Nothing beats a warm, freshly baked bagel. This recipe is for plain bagels, but you can add the toppings of your choice.

Cooking Time: 22 minutes

Servings: 6

Ingredients:

- 1 2/3 cups water
- 4 cups bread flour
- 1 tsp salt

- 3 tbsp. sugar
- 3 tbsp. canola oil
- 1 tbsp. instant yeast
- 10 cups water
- ¼ cup honey

Directions:

1. Add the water, flour, salt, sugar, oil and yeast to the bowl of a mixer.

2. Process at low speed for 8 minutes.

3. Place the dough in a bowl that is coated with oil.

4. Cover with plastic and let sit for 2 hours.

5. Punch the dough down.

6. Flour a flat surface and place the dough on it.

7. Punch it down and let rise for 2 hours.

8. Cut the dough into 6 pieces.

9. Roll each piece into a 6-inch sausage shape and create a circle.

10. Let the bagels sit for 20 minutes.

11. Preheat the oven to 475 degrees.

12. Cover a baking sheet with parchment paper.

13. Bring the water to boil in a pot and stir in the honey.

14. Place the bagels into the boiling water and let them cook 1 minutes, then flip and cook for another minute.

15. Use a slotted spoon to transfer the bagels to the baking sheet.

16. If you want to add toppings, now is the time to do so.

17. Bake for 20 minutes.

Jewish Rye Bread

Bread is the staff of life, and a good loaf of rye bread beats them all.

Cooking Time: 35 minutes

Servings: 12

Ingredients:

- 3 cups bread flour
- 1 ½ cup rye flour
- 1 tbsp. ground caraway seeds
- 2 tbsp. brown sugar

- 2 ½ tsp. instant yeast
- 2 tsp. salt
- ¼ cup canola oil
- 3 tbsp. sour pickle juice

Directions:

1. Place both flours, caraway seeds, brown sugar, yeast and salt in a mixer.

2. Use a low setting to combine the ingredients.

3. Stir together the oil, pickle juice with ¾ cup of water.

4. Add the oil to the flour mixture.

5. Continue mixing until you have a smooth dough.

6. Cover the dough with plastic and let sit for 30 minutes.

7. Knead the dough in the mixer for 8 minutes.

8. Flour a flat surface and continue kneading the dough for 2 minutes.

9. Coat a bowl with oil.

10. Create a dough ball and place the dough in the bowl.

11. Cover with plastic and let sit for 1 hour. The dough should be twice its size.

12. Lightly butter a 5 x 9 loaf pan.

13. Place the dough in the pan.

14. Cover with a damp cloth and let rise to twice its size, an hour to an hour and a half.

15. Preheat the oven to 350 degrees.

16. Place the pan in the oven and bake for 35 minutes.

Cinnamon Bread

This makes great toast in the morning. Smear with butter.

Cooking Time: 50 minutes

Servings: 10

Ingredients:

- 2 cups white flour
- 1 cup white sugar
- 1 tbsp. baking powder
- 1 cup raisins
- 2 tsp. cinnamon

- 1 cup milk
- 1 tbsp. vinegar
- 1 cup sour cream
- 2 eggs
- 1 tbsp. vanilla extract
- ½ tsp. baking soda
- ¼ cup brown sugar
- 2 tbsp. cinnamon

Directions:

1. Preheat the oven to 350 degrees.

2. Lightly butter a loaf pan.

3. Combine the flour, sugar, baking powder, baking soda, and cinnamon in a bowl.

4. In a second bowl, stir together the milk, vinegar, sour cream and vanilla.

5. Stir the milk mixture into the flour mixture.

6. Gently stir in the raisins.

7. Stir the brown sugar and cinnamon together.

8. Sprinkle the batter with the topping and swirl a knife to integrate into the batter.

9. Bake for 50 minutes.

Main Meals

Beef Brisket

This is soooo good, and yet easy to prepare. Just imagine those great sandwiches. In case you're wondering about the beer, it tenderizes the meat.

Cooking Time: 3 hours 30 minutes

Servings: 6

Ingredients:

- 3 lb. beef brisket
- Salt and pepper to taste
- 1 can of beer
- 12 oz. BBQ sauce
- 2 chopped garlic cloves
- 1 packet Lipton Onion Soup Mix
- ½ cup brown sugar

Directions:

1. Preheat the oven to 325 degrees.

2. Salt and pepper the brisket and place on a baking dish.

3. Combine the remaining ingredients in a bowl and pour over the meat.

4. Cover the baking dish with foil.

5. Bake for 3 hours and remove the foil.

6. Bake for 30 more minutes.

7. Slice the brisket and top with the gravy

Kosher Cholent Recipe

Cholen is as traditional for the Sabbath as matzo. It is slow-cooked overnight. You can also prepare cholen in the slow cooker

Cooking Time: 12 hours 40 minutes

Servings: 8

Ingredients:

- ¼ cup canola oil
- 2 chopped onions

- 3 minced garlic cloves
- 3 lb. chuck roast cut into large pieces
- 1 sliced kielbasa
- 2 cups kidney beans
- 1 cup pearl barley
- 5 peeled and quartered potatoes
- 5 cups chicken broth
- Salt and pepper to taste

Directions:

Heat the oil in a Dutch oven and sauté the onion and garlic for 5 minutes.

Add the beef and brown on all sides.

Add the kielbasa and beans and stir for 5 minutes.

Stir in the pearl barley and potatoes and chicken broth. Add water if necessary to cover the ingredients.

Bring the liquid to a boil.

Simmer for 30 minutes.

Preheat the oven to 200 degrees.

Cover the Dutch oven and transfer to the oven

Cook for 12 hours.

If needed, add more water.

Prime Rib

The perfect company or holiday meal. Serve with mashed potatoes

Cooking Time: 2 hours 10 minutes

Servings: 8

Ingredients:

- 4-lb prime rib roast
- 3 minced garlic cloves
- 1 tbsp. olive oil
- Salt and pepper to taste
- 1 tsp. thyme

- 1 tsp. rosemary
- 1 tsp. spicy mustard
- 1 cup Tofutti kosher sour cream
- 2 tbsp. horseradish
- Salt and pepper to taste

Directions:

1. Place the roast in a roasting pan.

2. Combine the garlic, oil, salt, pepper, thyme, rosemary and mustard in a bowl.

3. Coat the entire roast with the mixture and let sit for 1 hour.

4. Preheat the oven to 475 degrees.

5. Bake the roast for 20 minutes to sear in the juices.

6. Lower the temperature to 200 and cook for 1 ½ hours.

7. Check doneness with a meat thermometer. Medium rare will read 135 degrees.

8. Remove the roast from the oven and cover with foil for 20 minutes.

9. Combine the sour cream, horseradish, salt and pepper in a bowl.

10. Serve the sauce with the prime rib.

Slow Cooker Pot Roast

Perfect pot roast. Adding the vegetables halfway through the cooking process prevents them from getting mushy.

Cooking Time: 8 hours 5 minutes

Servings: 8

Ingredients:

- 4 lb. chuck roast
- Salt and pepper to taste
- ¼ tsp. garlic salt
- ¼ tsp. paprika

- 1 tbsp. olive oil
- 1 chopped onion
- 2 cups beef broth
- 1 tbsp. Worcestershire sauce
- 1 cup sliced mushrooms
- 1 bag baby carrots
- 3 peeled and cubed potatoes

Directions:

1. Season the roast with salt, pepper, garlic salt and paprika.

2. Drizzle the roast with the olive oil.

3. Brown the roast for 5 minutes each side.

4. Transfer the roast to the slow cooker and add the onion, broth and Worcestershire sauce.

5. Cook on low for 4 hours.

6. Toss in the vegetables and cook for another 4 hours

Roasted Chicken

Long before the rest of the world caught on, Jewish grandmothers were rubbing their Sabbath chicken with herbs. For a kosher chicken, be sure to use olive oil instead of butter.

Cooking Time: 2 hours

"To plant a garden is to believe in tomorrow."

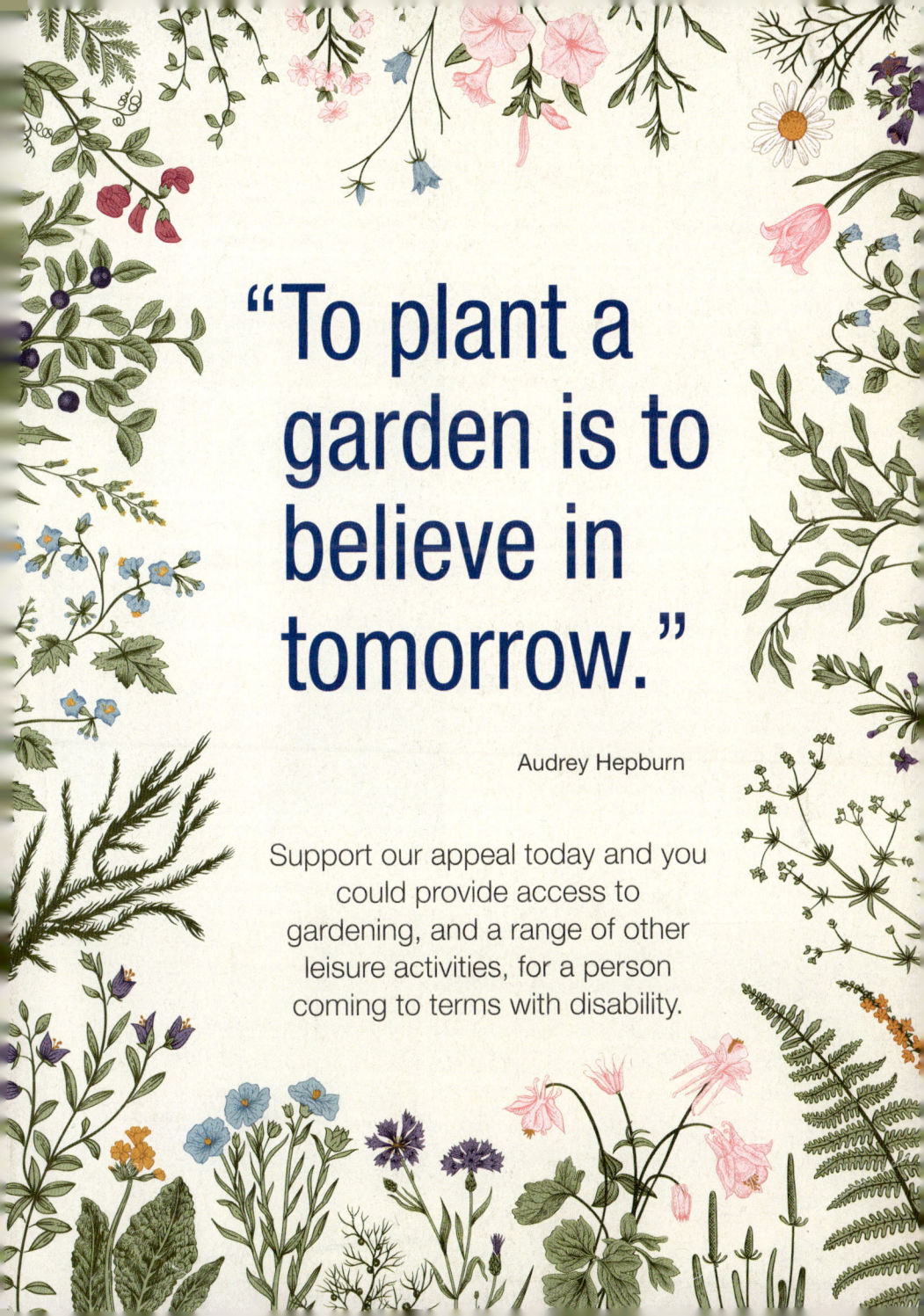

Audrey Hepburn

Support our appeal today and you could provide access to gardening, and a range of other leisure activities, for a person coming to terms with disability.

There are 1.2 million stroke survivors in the UK and two thirds of them will leave hospital with a disability

At the Royal Hospital for Neuro-disability (RHN) many of our patients are learning to cope with a disability due to a brain injury, like a stroke, or because they have a neurological condition like Huntington's Disease.

In a recent survey* more than three quarters of stroke survivors reported that their stroke had resulted in weakness in their arms.

Arm weakness can make it difficult for people to carry out daily living activities like getting dressed. It can also mean the hobbies and activities they once enjoyed, such as gardening, art or simply reading a book, become a lot more challenging.

*Stroke Association, February 2018

Leisure activities at the RHN

At the RHN, we pick up the pieces caused by strokes and other types of brain injury and help survivors start a second life living with disability. The dedicated staff and volunteers of our Leisure and Family Services (LAFS) team, facilitate a range of leisure activities for patients undergoing rehabilitation after a brain injury, and those in long term care.

Servings: 8

Ingredients:

- ¼ tsp. herbs de Provence
- ¼ tsp. rosemary
- ¼ tsp. tarragon
- ¼ tsp. thyme
- ¼ tsp. garlic powder
- Salt and pepper to taste
- 1 tbsp. lemon juice
- 3 tbsp. oil
- 3-lb. whole chicken
- 2 slices lemons
- 2 quartered onions
- 5 garlic cloves

Directions:

1. Preheat the oven to 350 degrees.

2. Combine all the herbs, spices, salt, pepper, lemon juice and olive oil in a bowl.

3. Rinse the chicken and place in a baking dish.

4. Rub the oil/herb mixture under the skin and on the outside and inside of the chicken.

5. Fill the chicken cavity with the lemons, onions and garlic.

6. Cook the chicken for 2 hours, until the juices run clear.

7. Remove the lemons, onions and garlic.

Cornish Game Hens

Not only are these game hens succulent and juicy, when arranged on a platter, they make a fabulous presentation. Count on one hen per person.

Cooking Time: 55 minutes

Servings: 4

Ingredients:

- 4 Cornish game hens
- Salt and pepper to taste

- 2 lemons
- 2 tbsp. olive oil
- 1 tsp. rosemary
- 1 tsp. poultry seasoning
- 10 sliced garlic cloves
- ¾ cup white wine
- ¾ cup chicken broth

Directions:

1. Preheat the oven to 450 degrees.

2. Combine the olive oil, salt, pepper, rosemary and poultry seasoning.

3. Rub the mixture all over the hens, including under the skin.

4. Fill the cavity of each hen with 2 lemon quarters.

5. Transfer the hens to a roasting pan.

6. Roast for 30 minutes.

7. Combine the garlic, wine and broth.

8. Pour the mixture over the hens.

9. Lower the heat to 350 degrees and cook for 25 minutes.

10. Baste the hens frequently during the last 25 minutes.

Turkey Breast in the Slow Cooker

Easy, delicious turkey. Just think of all those delicious turkey sandwiches!

Cooking Time:

Servings: 12

Ingredients:

- 6-lb. turkey breast
- 3 tbsp. butter
- ¼ tsp. oregano

- ¼ tsp. garlic salt
- Salt and pepper to taste
- ¼ tsp. thyme
- 4 chopped celery stalks
- 1 sliced onion
- 1 cup chicken broth

Directions:

1. Combine the butter with the oregano, garlic salt, salt, pepper and thyme.

2. Rub the mixture on the inside and outside of the turkey breast, including under the skin.

3. Please the celery stalks and onion in the slow cooker

4. Add the turkey breast.

5. Pour the chicken broth into the slow cooker.

6. Cook on low for 8 hours.

Stuffed Breast of Veal

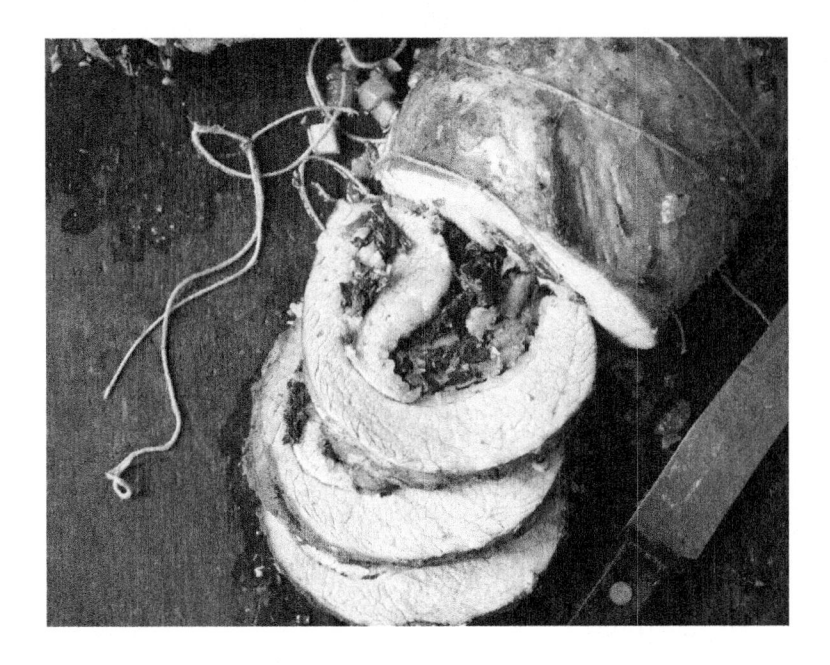

An old Jewish dish that is very impressive. Great for a holiday gathering.

Cooking Time: 3 hours 50 minutes

Servings: 12

Ingredients:

- 3 tbsp. olive oil
- 1 cup sliced mushrooms
- 1 cup chopped celery

- 1 cup chopped onion
- 3 minced garlic cloves
- 3 tbsp. chopped parsley
- 2 eggs from kosher hens
- ¼ cup chicken broth
- Salt and pepper to taste
- 7 cups croutons
- 5 lb. boneless breast of veal
- 1 tbsp. olive oil
- 1 tsp. paprika
- ¾ tsp. garlic powder
- ½ tsp sage
- salt and pepper to taste

Directions:

1. Preheat the oven to 400 degrees.

2. Heat the olive oil and sauté the mushrooms, onion, celery and garlic for 5 minutes. Set aside.

3. Whisk the eggs and chicken broth and add the croutons, parsley and sautéed vegetables and combine well.

4. Cut pockets into the breast of veal and fill with the stuffing mixture.

5. Transfer the veal breast to a roasting pan and cover with foil.

6. Cook for 3 ¾ hour while frequently basting with the drippings.

7. Remove the foil 30 minutes before the veal is done.

Breaded Veal Chops

Delicious. Quite similar to a German Schnitzel. The eggs are pareve, so they are allowed with the meat.

Cooking Time: 10 minutes

Servings 4:

Ingredients:

- 4 veal chops
- ½ cup breadcrumbs or matzo meal
- 2 beaten eggs

- ¼ canola oil
- Salt and pepper to taste
- ½ tsp. rosemary
- ½ tsp. garlic powder

Directions:

1. Place the eggs and breadcrumbs in 2 separate shallow dishes.

2. Add the seasoning to the breadcrumbs

3. Dredge the veal chops through the eggs, then the breadcrumbs.

4. Let the chops sit for 15 minutes.

5. Heat the oil in a skillet.

6. Fry the veal chops on low for 5 minutes each side.

7. Drain on a paper towel.

Soups and Stews

Matzo Ball Soup

This is the original comfort-food soup. It's worth getting a cold just to have someone prepare it. Note: If you are eating kosher, substitute lard or olive oil for the butter, as the combination butter (dairy) and meat does not work. You can also add noodles to the matzo balls for extra substance.

Cooking Time: 25 minutes

Servings: 10

Ingredients:

- 2 packages matzo crackers
- ½ cup butter
- 6 egg yolks
- 6 egg whites
- Salt and pepper to taste
- ¼ cup chopped parsley
- ¼ cup matzo meal
- 10 cups homemade chicken broth
- 2 diced onions
- 4 chopped celery stalks
- 4 sliced carrots
- ¼ cup chopped scallions

Directions:

1. Fill a soup pot with salted water and bring to a boil.

2. Chop the matzo crackers finely or process in a food processor.

3. Place them in a bowl and add just enough water to cover the crackers. Let soak for a few minutes.

4. Heat the butter in a skillet and stir in the soaked matzo and combine well.

5. Brown for 4 minutes.

6. Return the matzo to a bowl and add the egg yolks, salt, pepper and parsley.

7. Stir in the matzo meal.

8. Create golf ball size balls.

9. Place the matzo balls in the boiling water.

10. Wait until the matzo balls rise to the top. If they don't, start over with an extra egg.

11. Heat the chicken broth and add the onion, carrots, celery and scallion.

12. Let simmer for 20 minutes

13. Add the matzo balls to the broth.

Chicken Chili

Put a bit of spice in your life. This fantastic chili makes a great meal and a great use of left-over chicken. Serve it with a salad.

Cooking Time: 25 minutes

Servings: 8

Ingredients:

- 2 tbsp. olive oil
- 1 chopped onion
- 3 minced garlic cloves

- 2 cups chicken broth
- 1 ½ cup salsa verde
- 1 ½ cup canned chopped tomatoes
- 2 diced green chilis
- 1 cup fire-roasted tomatoes
- ½ tsp. oregano
- ¼ tsp. cumin
- 1 cup fresh corn kernels
- 1 lb. cubed cooked chicken
- 2 cups canned white beans
- Salt and pepper to taste

Directions:

1. Heat the olive oil in a pot and sauté the onion and garlic for 5 minutes.

2. Stir in the broth, salsa verde, tomatoes, chilis, fire-roasted tomatoes, oregano and cumin. Combine well.

3. Bring to a boil and simmer for 15 minutes.

4. Add the remaining ingredients.

5. Simmer for 10 minutes.

Sweet and Sour Cabbage Soup

A beloved Ashkenazi recipe. If you like, you can simmer beef or veal cubes in the broth.

Cooking Time: 1 hour 10 minutes

Servings: 10

Ingredients:

- 2 tbsp. olive oil
- 1 diced onion
- 1 tbsp. minced garlic
- 1 tbsp. sweet paprika

- 1 head chopped red cabbage
- 2 cups canned chopped tomatoes with juice
- 6 cups beef broth
- 3 tbsp. sugar
- 3 tbsp. cider vinegar
- Salt and pepper to taste

Directions

1. Heat the oil in a large pot.

2. Sauté the onion and garlic for 5 minutes.

3. Add the chopped cabbage and paprika and cook on low for 5 minutes.

4. Pour in the tomatoes and beef stock.

5. Stir well and let simmer for 1 hour.

6. Season with the sugar, vinegar, salt and pepper. Taste as you season.

7. Simmer for another 5 minutes.

Lentil Soup

This soup is insanely delicious and healthy. You can make it more substantial by adding a cup or two of shredded cooked chicken with the tomato and spinach.

Cooking Time: 1 hour 1 minute

Servings: 10

Ingredients:

- 2 cups dry lentils
- 10 cups chicken broth
- 2 cups tomato sauce

- 1 sliced onion
- 3 minced garlic cloves
- 2 tsp. cumin
- 3 peeled and sliced carrots
- 1 chopped tomato
- Bunch of baby spinach

Directions:

1. Combine all ingredients except the tomatoes and spinach in a large pot and simmer for 1 hour 15 minutes.

2. Keep on an eye on the liquid, which will be quickly absorbed by the lentils. Add more if needed.

3. Five minutes before the soup is done, stir in the tomatoes and spinach.

Seafood

Glazed Salmon

A snap to prepare, but definitely company-worthy

Cooking Time: 35 minutes

Servings: 4

Ingredients:

- ¼ cup honey
- 2 tbsp. soy sauce
- 2 tbsp. Dijon mustard
- 2 tbsp. whiskey

- 4 salmon fillets
- Salt and pepper to taste

Directions:

1. Preheat the oven to 375 degrees.

2. Cover a baking dish with aluminum foil.

3. Combine the honey, soy sauce, mustard and whiskey in a bowl.

4. Season the salmon with salt and pepper.

5. Brush each fillet with the glazing mixture.

6. Bake for 35 minutes, until the salmon is flaky.

Halibut with Walnut Coating

A simple but tasty way to enjoy fish. If you aren't concerned about keeping kosher, you can substitute butter for the coconut oil. But the coconut oil is extremely healthy.

Cooking Time: 10 minutes

Servings: 6

Ingredients:

- ¼ cup Dijon mustard
- ¼ cup coconut oil

- 3 tsp. honey
- ¼ tsp. garlic powder
- ½ cup breadcrumbs
- ½ cup chopped walnuts
- 1 tbsp. chopped parsley
- Salt and pepper to taste
- 6 halibut fillets

Directions:

1. Preheat the oven to 400 degrees.

2. Combine the mustard, coconut oil, honey and garlic powder in a bowl.

3. Chill for 15 minutes.

4. Combine the breadcrumbs, walnuts and parsley.

5. Salt and pepper the halibut fillets.

6. Top first with the mustard mixture, then with the breadcrumbs.

7. Bake for 10 minutes, until the fillets are flaky.

Exotic Shabbat Fish

The flavors are incredible. You want plenty of Challah to soak up the broth. Serve with a Pareve yogurt sauce.

Cooking Time: 25 minutes

Servings: 6

Ingredients:

- 1 red bell pepper, cut into thin strips
- 4 small sliced tomatoes
- 6 cod fillets

- 2 tbsp. paprika
- 1 tbsp. Lebanese 7-Spice Blend (Check your supermarket or online)
- ½ tsp. cayenne pepper
- Salt and pepper to taste
- 1/3 cup fish broth

Directions:

1. Place the bell pepper and tomato slices in a large skillet.

2. Top with the fish fillets.

3. In a bowl, combine the paprika, Lebanese 7-Spices, salt, pepper, broth with a cup of water.

4. Spoon the sauce over the fish.

5. Cover the skillet and cook on low for 25 minutes, or until the cod is flaky and the vegetables are done.

Sides

Roasted Cauliflower

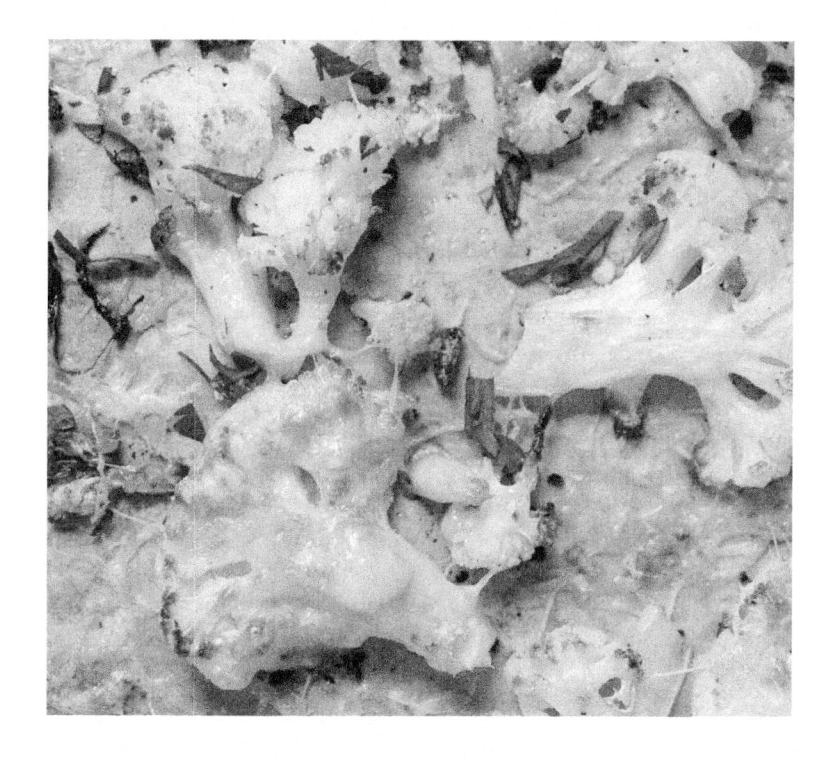

This side dish will complement just about anything. So simple, yet so tasty.

Cooking Time: 30 minutes

Servings: 6

Ingredients:

- 3 minced garlic cloves
- ¼ cup of grated Parmesan cheese
- 3 tbsp. olive oil
- 1 cauliflower cut into florets
- Black pepper and Salt to taste

Directions:

1. Preheat the oven to 450 degrees.

2. Coat a baking sheet with non-stick spray

3. Coat the cauliflower with the olive oil (placing both in a plastic bag and shaking works great.

4. Transfer the florets to the baking dish.

5. Season with salt and pepper.

6. Bake for 20 minutes.

7. Drizzle with the cheese and bake for another 10 minutes.

Cheese Blintzes

These can be a snack or a side dish.

Cooking Time: 16 minutes

Servings: 5

Ingredients

- 4 eggs
- 1 ¼ flour
- ¾ cup milk
- ½ cup water
- 2 tbsp. sugar
- Dash of vanilla extract

- 1 cup mascarpone cheese
- 1 cup cream cheese
- ½ tsp. lemon extract
- 3 egg yolks
- 3 tbsp. sugar
- Dash of salt
- 1 tbsp. canola oil
- 3 tbsp. butter

Directions:

1. Add the eggs, flour, milk, water, salt and vanilla in a blender and combine until smooth.

2. Set aside for 30 minutes.

3. Combine the mascarpone, cream cheese, lemon extract, egg yolk, vanilla and salt in a bowl.

4. Refrigerate for 1 hour.

5. Heat 1 tbsp. oil in a skillet.

6. Use ¼ cup of batter for each blintz.

7. Keep moving the skillet around as the blintz browns for 1 minute.

8. Flip to the other side and cook another minute.

9. Repeat with the entire batter. Keep the crepes warm.

10. Preheat the oven to 325 degrees.

11. Lightly butter a baking dish.

12. Fill each crepe with about ¼ cup of cheese filling.

13. Roll the crepe up and secure the sides.

14. Heat the butter in a skillet and brown the blintzes 2 minutes per side.

15. Arrange the browned blintzes in the baking dish.

16. Bake for 12 minutes.

17. Top to confectioner's sugar or a fruit sauce.

Passover Haroset

This is a traditional Seder dish going back to Egyptian times.

Cooking Time: 0

Servings: 6

Ingredients:

- 6 apples
- ½ cup chopped pecans
- ½ cup chopped almonds
- ½ tsp. cinnamon
- 2 tbsp. honey

- ¼ cup red wine

Directions:

1. Core the apples and grate them in a food processor.

2. Combine the grated apples, pecans, almonds, cinnamon and honey.

3. Drizzle in the wine and toss.

Potato Latkes

The secret to perfect latkes is to drain as much liquid out of the grated potatoes as possible so that they crisp. A cheesecloth works well. Pro Tip: shredding the potatoes is less work but grating them improves the texture tremendously. Worth the effort.

Cooking Time: 10 minutes

Servings: 4

Ingredients:

- 2 cups grated potatoes
- 2 tbsp. grated onion
- 1 beaten egg
- 3 tbsp. matzo meal
- 3 tbsp. chopped scallions
- Salt and pepper to taste
- ½ cup canola oil

Directions:

1. Combine all ingredients except the oil.

2. Form potatoes patties no thicker than ¼ inch.

3. Heat the oil in a skillet.

4. Fry 5 minutes on one side on low heat, then turn and fry the other side for 5 minutes.

5. Drain the latkes on a paper towel.

6. Serve with sour cream and applesauce.

Beans and Artichoke Salad

This refreshing salad is served at a lot of Seder dinners.

Cooking Time: 0

Servings: 8

Ingredients:

- 2 cups drained cannellini beans
- 12 oz. quartered and drained artichoke hearts
- ¼ cup chop Kalamata olives
- 1 chopped onion
- ¼ cup chopped parsley

- 2 tbsp. chopped arugula
- 2 tbsp. chopped basil
- 1/3 cup olive oil
- 2 tbsp. red wine vinegar
- 1 tsp. lemon juice
- salt and pepper to taste
- ¼ cup feta cheese

Directions:

1. Toss the beans, artichokes, olives, onion, parsley, arugula and basil in a salad bowl.

2. Combine the olive oil, vinegar and lemon juice.

3. Season the salad with salt and pepper.

4. Drizzle with the dressing.

5. Top with feta cheese.

Herring Salad

Herring salad and a bagel make a fine meal. For ease of preparation, buy pickled herring at the supermarket. Because the herring is processed and cured, you can use sour cream and remain kosher. Just make sure your herring is pareve.

Cooking Time: 0

Servings: 6

Ingredients:

- 14 oz. chopped jarred herring
- 1 chopped onion
- 1 peeled and chopped apples
- 1 cup left-over cubed potatoes
- 3 tbsp. chopped parsley
- 2 tbsp. cider vinegar
- ¼ cup sour cream
- Salt and pepper taste
- 2 tbsp. chopped dill

Directions:

1. Toss the herring, onion, apples, potatoes in a bowl.

2. Combine the cider vinegar, sour cream in a bowl.

3. Stir the sour cream into the herring mixture.

4. Season with salt and pepper and top with dill.

Dessert

Rugelach

Delicious little bits of pastry. You can be creative with the filling.

Cooking Time: 25 minutes

Servings: 45

Ingredients:

- 1 cup butter
- 1 package cream cheese
- 2 cups flour
- Dash of salt

- 1/2 cup white sugar
- 1 tbsp. cinnamon
- 1 cup finely chopped walnuts
- 1 cup chocolate chips
- 1 tsp. vanilla extract

Directions:

1. Place the butter, cream cheese, flour and sour cream in a food processor and process to a crumbly consistency.

2. Create 4 equal-sized disks and refrigerate for at least 12 hours.

3. Combine the sugar, cinnamon, walnuts, chocolate chips and vanilla extract and process.

4. Roll a disk into a 1/8 inch thickness.

5. Coat each disk with the nut filling

6. Repeat with remaining disks.

7. Use a sharp knife to cut each disk with 12 wedges.

8. Dust a flat surface with sugar.

9. Roll the dough wedges starting from the wide end.

10. Place the rugelach on a baking sheet and refrigerate for 30 minutes.

11. Preheat the oven to 350 degrees.

12. Bake for 25 minutes.

Chocolate Torte

This is perfect for Passover. This is perfectly kosher. If you are okay with non-kosher, just use chocolate chips instead of the cocoa powder, coconut oil and sugar.

Cooking Time:

Servings: 12

Ingredients:

- ½ cup pareve margarine
- 6 tbsp. cocoa powder
- 1 cup coconut oil

- 1 cup sugar
- 5 egg yolks
- 5 egg whites
- ¾ cup white sugar
- 1 cup ground almonds
- 1 cup warmed raspberry sauce

Directions:

1. Preheat the oven to 350 degrees.

2. Line a springform pan with aluminum foil.

3. Melt the margarine, cocoa powder, coconut oil and sugar in a pan until it is smooth.

4. Whisk the egg whites in one bowl.

5. In a second bowl, whisk the egg yolks and ¾ cup sugar.

6. Combine the cocoa mixture, egg yolks and ground almonds.

7. Fold the egg whites into the mixture.

8. Transfer the batter to the spring form pan.

9. Fill a baking sheet with an inch of water and add the spring form pan.

10. Bake for 45 minutes.

11. Cover the cake with foil during the last 15 minutes.

12. Let cook and drizzle with raspberry sauce.

Apple Bundt Cake

This is a classic dessert following a holiday meal.

Cooking Time: 1 hour

Servings: 12

Ingredients:

- ½ cup brown sugar
- ½ cup canola oil
- ½ cup applesauce
- 2 eggs
- ½ cup honey

- 1 tsp. vanilla extract
- 2 ½ cups white flour
- 1 tsp. baking powder
- ½ tsp. salt
- 1 tsp. cinnamon
- ½ tsp nutmeg
- 3 shredded apples
- ½ tsp. baking soda
- 2/3 cup chopped walnuts

Directions:

1. Preheat the oven to 325 degrees.

2. Grease a 9-inch Bundt pan.

3. Combine the brown sugar, oil, apple sauce, eggs, honey and vanilla extract.

4. In another bowl, combine the baking powder, flour, baking soda, cinnamon and nutmeg.

5. Stir the flour mix into the sugar mixture.

6. Add the apples and nuts.

7. Place the batter in the Bundt pan.

8. Bake for 1 hour but check for doneness around 45 minutes.

Kugel

Very traditional Jewish holiday dessert. Sweet and buttery.

Cooking Time: 1 hour

Servings: 8

Ingredients:

- 1 package cooked large egg noodles
- ¼ cup butter
- 6 eggs
- ½ cup white sugar
- 2 cups sour cream
- 2 ½ cups cottage cheese
- 1 pinch salt

- 3 tbsp. softened butter
- 3 tbsp. sugar
- 1 tsp. cinnamon
- 2/3 cup crushed cornflakes

Directions:

1. Preheat the oven to 350 degrees.

2. Coat a 9x13 baking dish with non-stick spray.

3. Stir the butter into the cooked noodles.

4. Whip together the eggs, sugar and sour cream.

5. Add the buttered noodles, cottage cheese and salt.

6. Place the noodle mixture in the baking dish.

7. Combine the butter, sugar, cinnamon and cornflakes in a bowl.

8. Layer the cornmeal mixture on top of the noodles.

9. Bake for 1 hour 1 hour.

Honey Cake

This is a Rosh Hashanah tradition.

Cooking Time: 1 hour

Servings: 10

Ingredients:

- 3 ½ cups white flour
- 1 tbsp. baking powder
- 1 tsp. of baking soda
- 2 tbsp. cinnamon
- 1 tsp. nutmeg

- 1 cup vegetable oil
- ¼ tsp. salt
- ¾ cup honey
- ½ cup molasses
- ¾ cup white sugar
- ¼ cup brown sugar
- 3 eggs
- 1 tsp. orange extract
- 1 cup strong coffee
- 1/3 cup orange juice
- ¼ cup rum
- ¼ cup confectioner's sugar

Directions:

1. Preheat your oven to 350 degrees.

2. Coat a tube pan with non-stick spray.

3. Combine the flour, baking powder, baking soda, salt, cinnamon and nutmeg in a bowl.

4. Whisk together the oil, honey, molasses, both sugars, eggs, orange extract, coffee, orange juice and rum in another bowl.

5. Whip the flour into the honey mixture.

6. Transfer the batter to the tube pan.

7. Bake for 1 hour.

8. Dust with confectioner's sugar.

9. Let cool before slicing.

Printed in Great Britain
by Amazon